Range of Light

POEMS

CATHARINE SAVAGE BROSMAN

LOUISIANA STATE UNIVERSITY PRESS

BATON ROUGE

Published by Louisiana State University Press
Copyright © 2007 by Catharine Savage Brosman
All rights reserved
Manufactured in the United States of America
An LSU Press Paperback Original
FIRST PRINTING

DESIGNER: *Amanda McDonald Scallan*
TYPEFACE: *Whitman*
PRINTER AND BINDER: *Edwards Brothers, Inc.*

Library of Congress Cataloging-in-Publication Data

Brosman, Catharine Savage, 1934–
     Range of light : poems / Catharine Savage Brosman.
     p. cm.
     ISBN-13: 978-0-8071-3216-6 (pbk. : alk. paper)
     I. Title.
PS3552.R666R36 2007
813'.54—dc22

                                                    2006010537

Grateful acknowledgment is made to the editors of the following publications, in which poems herein appeared earlier: *American Scholar:* "Cholla"; *Anglican Theological Review:* "A Taos Hymn"; *Chronicles: A Magazine of American Culture:* "At Bishop's Lodge," "Blue Spruce, Santa Fé," "Indian Paintbrush," "The Narrows"; *The Claflin Review:* "Potsherds"; *The Classical Outlook:* "Mud-pots"; *Crisis: Politics, Culture, and the Church:* "Raspberries"; *Critical Quarterly:* "Aspen in a Burn," "Canyon Wrens," "Joshua Trees," "Stratton's Gold"; *Desire Street:* "Great Sand Dunes," "Petroglyphs"; *Jubilee: A Festival of the Arts and Humanities at Nicholls State University:* "Sunset, with Red Rain"; *Louisiana Literature:* "At Los Gallos," "Grand Staircase"; *The Lyric:* "In the Wind River Range," "Mesquite"; *Méasŭre:* "Moon on the Conejos River"; *New Delta Review:* "Prickly Pear"; *Sewanee Review:* "Bristlecone Pines," "Frémont in California," "Frémont in the Granite Range," "La Glorieta"; *Smartish Pace:* "Painted Desert," "Stillwater Marsh"; *Snowy Egret:* "Plums"; *South Carolina Review:* "Blue Herons," "Georgia's Ladders," "Ghost Ranch," "Great Pine"; *Southern Humanities Review:* "In the Abajo Mountains," "Llano Estacado," "Moraine," "Sage"; *Southern Review:* "Conejos Rising," "Enos Mills on the Divide," "Kachinas," "Weavings"; *Southwest Review:* "In the Zuni Lands"; *Weber Studies:* "Dust Devil," "Snow in Taos"; *Xavier Review:* "Sand Paintings." "Indian Paintbrush" and "Sunset, with Red Rain" were republished in *The Book of Irish American Poetry from the 18th Century to the Present,* ed. Daniel Tobin (South Bend: University of Notre Dame Press, 2007). "Sunset, with Red Rain" also appeared in *Poetry Calendar 2005,* © 2004 Alhambra Publishing. Some poems in this collection appeared also in my chapbook *Petroglyphs: Poems and Prose,* privately printed by Jubilee: A Festival of the Arts and Humanities at Nicholls State University (Thibodaux, La., 2003).

To my daughter and son-in-law, Kate and Brian Deimling, with love, and in memory of two cherished people: my father, Paul Victor Hill (1907–1969), of whom I can say *(n'en déplaise à Montaigne):* ". . . *le meilleur père qui fût onques*"; and Evelyn Powell Payne (1935–2001), a devoted friend for forty-nine years: "*Par ce que c'estoit [elle], par ce que c'estoit moy.*"

"C'est une absolue perfection, et comme divine, de scavoyr jouyr loiallement de son estre" [It is absolute perfection, and as if divine, to know how to enjoy one's being properly].

—MONTAIGNE

Contents

Range of Light

From Colorado, we had reeled ourselves out, south
and west, to the Navajo lands, looping through
the Lukachukai Mountains down to Chinle
and Canyon de Chelly, thence, after a few days
under cottonwoods, north to Kayenta and Monument
Valley, where we camped as in a sea-trough,

treeless, among the sandstone pinnacles—dolmens
of the wind; and each day, transparency of thought
to the vast horizon, its distances bleached out
as the curving earth yielded no more; and, purer
than any water, the blue-flame sky, burning
scarlet, gold, sienna, rose at sunset. Crossing

into Utah, still without shade, we had driven
to the Goosenecks of the San Juan River, picnicked
at the overlook, then visited the arching paradigms
of Natural Bridges and rested on cool stone.
Backtracking east, we stopped in Blanding,
where at closing time in the state liquor store we got

a bottle of their finest wine; then, at Monticello,
we turned west again, into the pod of the Abajos
breaching the plateau. The road ascended straight—
three, four thousand feet—and we climbed
the cresting waves in second gear. Sparse piñon pine
gave way to stands of aspen, fir, and spruce,

tossing sprays of mellowed light; I could imagine
druids taking refuge there, or dryads fleeing
from the desert noon. We found a campsite
near a brook, where two deer drank at dusk,
with groves of aspen and young pines, masts
and rigging bending in the wind, and long shafts

of sun-motes dappling us, as if it were a Gothic
chapel, or a Gaudí nave, all marvel and emotion,
textured leafily. Day melted down, flowing
into darkness, and the fading sky turned on
its beacon stars. We built a fire and, around
the branching flames, raised glasses of the Cabernet,

a mediocre toast to our imperfect being. Later,
as we huddled in the chill, embers glowing
in the circle of hot stones, then whitening to ash,
it seemed that we had caught ourselves, mind
becoming what it held a moment: space,
tree, mountain, fire—the journey and its end as one.

MUD-POTS

—Yellowstone Park

This must be an inferno, not the earth,
with Stygian spirits, wakened in their holes,
emerging in a great primeval birth—
hot mud-pots, geysers, pools, and fumaroles.

From underneath the crust the magma boils,
then, breaking, bubbles, gurgles, swirls, and fumes,
while the confusion of the crosswinds roils
the steam, and geysers, rumbling, rise in plumes;

and calcine waters gushing from the springs
form terraced pits, fantastic, as they flow,
with ferrous residue creating rings
and mineral wounds that bleed against the snow.

At the horizon, azure mountains wave,
uplayered past the foreground evergreen,
which hood their stillness, sapient and grave.
The mirror of mind is double—hills, serene,

and this unholy show of molten stuff:
the smells are foul, the pots are ghastly, strange,
and fascination cannot get enough,
while eyes conspire on the mountain range—

as Dante with his guide among the shades
watched, horrified, the wicked writhe in pain,
then, underground, returned to starry glades,
and visited in dream a higher plane,

which led him to the realm of Paradise,
where in a vision he saw Beatrice—
the daystar bursting rose in sacrifice,
the burden of the world transformed to bliss.

MORAINE

These are the runes of time, these stones.
Their roughness all is gone: as round and smooth
as beads, and speckled like a bird's egg,
they collect, washed clean, in cairns or cryptic
patterns on the river's breast, and sparkle
in the shallows where the ripples
yield to clear serenity. Feel: they've gathered

sun, the way my memory will keep this moment.
Yet their heart is frozen as the glaciers
that reformed their rougher truth. One year
we rode the rapids of the Snake,
a foursome most unusual—the very old,
the young, the middling; but we all
were children then, joining the water as it gave

its laughter to that journey, with its rushing
sounds, its babble, and the dazzling
light that played upon the foam, the rocks. Did
we feel then how the cold would come
again, and how our lives would fall
to pieces—flotsam, flesh undone, as nothing
to the mountain's movement? Afterwards,

I wanted to go sleep among the stones,
and lose myself in earth. The writing scatters
past the shore, into the wind. With what
is left, after the maelstrom, I would wish
a spirit chastened, smoothed,
—reflecting blue of sky and gray of granite, dry,
and hard, and enigmatic as a bone.

Where flames devoured it in an avalanche,
this broad swathe on a mountainside was scarred,
incinerated by the winds of chance,
its underbrush consumed, its timber charred.

The aspen, though, are moving back, the shoots
emerging through the blackened soil and ash
from serpentine adventure of new roots,
which have the run of earth's tenebrous cache.

A forest harbinger, a willing probe
for conifers, they herald spruce and fir,
to prosper later in full-needled robe
and emulate their fellows' white hauteur.

With tender parchment bark, pale verdigris,
and armaments of petiole and blade,
young trunks of aspen breach the fire's debris,
aspiring higher toward their future shade,

when supple limbs will fan the rippling light
to dapple artfully the painted ground—
each leaf alert to quiver at each sleight
of motion purposing an airy sound—

and shelter cinquefoil, columbine, and fern,
whose seeds and spores, concealed, were still alive
or, blowing, scattered winged thoughts on the burn
which in the aspens' shadow bloom and thrive—

till drying treetops turn to autumn gold,
pieces of eight among the evergreen,
then shake their wealth, preparing for the cold,
when bones alone become the snowy scene.

IN THE WIND RIVER RANGE

The wind breathes huskily along this range,
which cuts the continent and shapes the skies;
the brilliant shadings of the mountains change
to passion where Sacajawea lies.

This was the wilderness, replete and free,
a dream of nature, reaching from the plain,
through eminence of forests, to the sea,
resplendent spirit of its own domain.

She had been taken in the autumn snow
and traded to a Mandan; sold again
to be a wife of Toussaint Charbonneau,
conversant in the tongue of whiter men.

And she, Bird Woman, guided them and told
of waters higher still and distant crests,
then dazzling rivers farther down, which flowed
as foamy expectation in their breasts.

At Lemhi Pass, they crossed the Great Divide,
then traveled through the Bitterroots and found
those westward waters running to the tide,
the vastest prospects and the deepest sound.

Against the memory of sky and cloud,
I see them silhouetted as they climb,
their faces shaded now as by a shroud,
their fingers linked to lead them into time.

A ghostly presence mourns around her grave;
the wind, which gathers fury through the pass,
stirs up the ardent sand, and aspen wave
farewell to what departed with the grass.

The enterprise was risky from the start;
but I was young, and mountains gave delight
and pride. High at the sources of the Grand,
my collie, Scotch, and I, in winter's heart,
had camped on glaciers and explored the dark
and shaggy pelts of frozen woods. We then
began our awful climb to the Divide.
This was despite the signs of blizzard—herds

of heavy clouds collecting on the peaks,
the sky oppressive as an iron lid,
a darting tongue of turbulence, with snow
already deep, defending treacherous slopes
and battlements a thousand feet above.
We had not eaten for a day and dared
not wait for better weather. To descend
the western side, deserted, seemed unwise;

the crest, though, was not far, then Estes Park
and home. The flakes swirled round with dervish rage
through light almost crepuscular; my feet
in snowshoes and my clothing turning white,
I had become an animal, transformed
by its surroundings. As we picked our way
near timberline, the hunchback, shipwrecked trees
were swallowed by the drifts, which disappeared

in turn where gales dissolved the snow to dust.
Across a bare plateau, we met the ridge
of the Divide, its crags like canine teeth,
with gorges in between. I tied my dog
to me. We alternately climbed and slid
together; several times my hand-holds slipped
and in a rush of rock and ice we fell.
By nightfall, we were struggling still. Congealed

with cold, I carved a snowdrift cave, unrolled
my elk-skin sleeping bag well back, and Scotch
crawled in, then I. Next day, the worst remained:
a wall of granite, nearly vertical
and icy, with no footholds. *I* could climb,
with tools, but Scotch? I had to carry him,
and cut my way at the same time. He let
me sling him, sack-like, on one shoulder. As

I worked, the whirling winds exploded, hissed,
and roared in waves of force. A breaker hit;
we slipped and almost tumbled into space,
Scotch falling on me as I held somehow,
my feet, prehensile, wedged in chiseled holes
below. Some minutes later, we had reached
the summit's point, in sun. It was a birth
of consciousness: a continent spread out,

broad-winged, two oceans of a brilliant white,
and I, embracing them, the only mind.
There is no fathoming of being—ours
a moment, absolutely, either all
or nothing; yet I felt it to the depths—
such empty air, such plenitude of peaks
that body, molting, seemed to drop away,
and snowy thought became the snowy world.

We've taken pains to get here, fording the broad
San Luis Valley, with its cottonwoods
and streams, its fields of vegetables and hay,
then turning north, leaving behind all other purposes.
A long drive advances thought toward the rampart
of the Sangre de Cristos and the dunes. Of

course, there's a visitor center, with displays,
a bookshop, slide show, and cold drinks—since,
in human terms, this is for our enjoyment.
The road then curls, descending to a line of willows
and small desert plants, which edge a riverbed
of undulating sand, waving off beyond the trees,

its shallow pools alive with images of sky.
On the other side begin the dunes, immense, arising
incommensurate above the strand—ochre,
almost rose. Sandals off, we wet our feet a bit,
and watch a sprinkling of children dash
about, printing the pliant earth, wading in glee,

venturing out mid-stream ahead of parents, trousers
rolled, who run to catch them, all then
struggling up the slopes. The dunes remain
unmoved by shrieks and laughter, bodies bending
in the climb, in complaint, and unmoved
by gaze or admiration—waiting on the southwest

wind, which drives them toward the mountains,
where they press against the rocky flanks,
until a northeast gale remands them back
upon themselves, riffling, cresting in a Chinese wall.
Suddenly, some Amish visitors appear,
the men in black and bearded—hot, you'd think,

but shaded by those hats—the women bonneted,
in dresses of another age, the children quaintly
garbed. How did they get here, to release their awe
with ours? Curious, their exile in this world
of pleasure and machines; and strange,
the motions of the sands, their power, their barren

purity. Day is a sieve, hours running through;
already, light turns westerly and angles
long, composing shadows on the dunes' far face.
The winds come galloping again, shaping
the valley dust into a new creation, casting
about for us—such relics to be written in the runes.

INDIAN PAINTBRUSH

To paint the western steppe, get rabbit-brush
and choose a palette: dusty blue, gray, green,
for sage and grasses, waving in a rush
of jester wind that plays across the scene;

next, yellow, lavender, and prairie white,
for primrose, hopsage, prickly pear in bloom;
and last, apply the brilliant carmine light
of Indian paintbrush, brandishing its plume.

In artistry, each petal, leaf, and bract
provides, by serendipitous design,
enticement—eye and insect drawn to fact
of cunning chemistry incarnadine.

Its flowers fit the tongue of hummingbird
that hovers by invisible decree;
the style and stamens shoot a verdant word
beside the sepals' scarlet poetry.

Resourceful, though a facultative guest,
it takes its beauty from the sagebrush root,
both parasite and ornament. The rest
is sun and rain and Kokopelli's flute,

which whistles from the mesa tops to lead
imagination past the summer blaze,
and scatters glyphs of memory that bleed
among the playa stones in grief and praise.

STRATTON'S GOLD

—Colorado, 1896

The fire, raging under bull-whip winds
that lashed at Cripple Creek in springtime freeze,
consumed the dance hall, then stampeded on
throughout the camp, destroying everything.
The wrecked survivors felt the vise of cold
as it hit zero, with the children wrapped
in cindered rags, and women losing warmth,
exhausted. Stratton had found luck with gold—

desire, motive, mistress, charily
revealing flashes of herself—but not
the prize, until he'd hit a vein that ran
for forty feet in Independence mine,
and wealth was his, a million in a year,
then more. And yet he'd kept his ways—his friends
in prospecting, his mountain cabin, work,
at night some whiskey. Others—Tabor, Bell,

and Wheeler—bought, with fortune, women, rank,
and fame; but Stratton didn't change. How rare,
a man disdaining riches as his god
for honor and display: it was the search
he wanted—courtship, hunting, challenge. When
the fire came, the mayor at the Springs,
alerted, said he could do nothing; let
the miners take their own in hand. One did:

he had a train made up and ordered beef,
canned milk and beans, and bread; he cleared the stores
of blankets; clothes and children's things were brought
and loaded; tents were fetched. Two boxcars, filled,
rolled up Ute Pass that night to Cripple Creek.
By torchlight, wagons hauled the goods above
the reservoir, where families crouched, and men
erected tents and opened crates; the gold

from Stratton's hands flowed into theirs, as fires,
a blessing this time, heated food and hearts.
And later, in the city, he gave out
a fortune, lighting others' lives. His own
was plain: one servant and a manager,
yet still seemed incommensurate with dream,
and lucre alien, since he had lost
the days of riding burro-back along

a trail, of panning streams and placer mines
alone and working claims the way one works
a thought, its possibilities a lode—
assaying dawn rosaceous on the peak,
the scent of pines at night, blue columbine
with scarlet gilia beside a brook,
and ore of thunderclouds releasing rain,
then breaking into bright moraines of sun.

CONEJOS RISING

For Patricia J. Teed

The river's not yet crested, says the handsome fellow
from the Water Board—pressed jeans and boots,
a fine square jaw and resonant baritone—who's here
to warn us that the floodgates at Platoro Reservoir
have just been opened to relieve the pressure on the dam.
Each day we've watched the river, checking
hourly by rough measures, trying to assess the flow—
a large branch at the edge, besieged; the bridge, its arches

licked, devoured; a shoal of river stones, deluged—
but the turbulence confounds us, rushing, eddying,
defying all precision. Twenty-three hundred cfs—nearly
flood stage—at the Mogote gauge, with new melt
oozing from the snow pack, gathering speed,
steeping off, fluming, cutting and slaloming down
the slopes. And now more. I can understand
Heraclitus brooding on time's steady stream—recurring

constantly, never identical. What about experience
that overflows? The river's our familiar, so alive, robust,
with the current pulsing, sunlight faceted along
its surface, then shadowy for sleep; yet it's alien—a lover
to be wary of.—Time's slipping by for both
of us, good friend, as if we were rappelling down
a rock face; but we've got a gorgeous view on life
from here: Engelmann spruce, aspen higher up, a lodge

nudging the ridge, the long prospect of your grandfather,
"the Deacon," lover of horses, mountains, women,
who from a roll of thousand-dollar bills drew ten,
the legend says, to buy this property. "The disappearing
moment of experience is the firmest reality."
That's from a musician. The river's fugue runs on,
chasing its desire; we wave to the ephemeral,
imagining Deacon's voice: "Now, mine the lode, love now."

MOON ON THE CONEJOS RIVER

Full moon, full river now—a mountain tide
at flood stage and still rising with the flow
released from fortress peaks of the Divide,
where spring subverts high parapets of snow.

Careening from Platoro Reservoir,
the river seeps through meadows, undermines
its banks, invades low thickets, leaves a scar
among uprooted willows, sodden pines,

and bears as casual trophies limbs and boughs
that ride the current, catch, turn, plunge, and rush,
white-watering on rapids where it plows
against a weir of river stones and brush.

Serene, the moonlight multiplies, and makes
a thousand-mirrored mosaic on the stream,
a shifting coat of mail, as armor breaks,
then links again in images of dream—

a silvered knowledge showering the world—
in emulation of prehensile mind,
whose luminosity, reflected, pearled,
discloses in phenomena one kind,

embracing perfect moments and debris—
the swift inscription of a night-bird's arc,
the inundated grass, a floating tree,
unearthly music playing to the dark.

BLUE HERONS

They're cosmopolitan, these great blue herons,
gracefully adaptable and with eclectic
appetites, flourishing beneath the oaks and Spanish
moss that canopy Louisiana bayous, nesting in the pines
along the Sabine River at Toledo Bend
and by the sea-oat dunes of Matagorda. Even
in the Rockies, with high avian ways inscribed in spruce

and aspen—mountain bluebirds, owls, and chickadees—
the herons thrive, in colonies on sandbars
of the Colorado River as it flattens, widens, rests
after its mountain rush, catching its breath between
Grand Mesa, to the south, and, northward,
the White River Forest. As we take an s-curve, folded
in the gorge the way a heron bends its neck

in flight, here's one at the river's edge, in bluish
plumage, black lapels and crest and snowy crown,
as dignified as any New York *maître d'*.
The order of the day is azure sheets aloft for summer
sailing, down-edged cirrus tacking in the wind,
and water playing washboard on the stones or strumming
reeds and willows. The Latins called the heron

ardea, and this one is *herodias*—in homage
to its courtship dance, its smoky vanes arranged in veils,
transforming light and shadow into blue desire.
Downstream, two herons wade in shallows, feeding.
Suddenly, a flash of movement mirrored,
as a dagger bill harpoons its prey. Another heron
flushes up, its long legs trailing, wingbeats slow

and elegant. I feel myself slide out with it along
air currents, thought becoming strangely feathered
and unworded, as I glide above the heronry
into another valence, higher still, hearing an aery cry,
knowing in my wings how killing, loving, flying, being, all
are one—nothing beyond the act, the moment
and awareness fitting smoothly, dense and crystalline.

Snow blanches the range, rounding arroyos,
planing the rough sagebrush, frosting
juniper and piñon pine scattered like embroidery
on an altar cloth. Few are on the road with me
this winter afternoon, since storms rode in yesterday
to set up camp in the Sangre de Cristos:
winds hurling themselves at the cabin walls, cold

reaching into windows, mocking the blankets,
drifts forming silently in the night, ice coming to be.
I had to leave, however. Driving down
from Colorado, rising over one pass, two,
I horseshoed, looped, and felt my way
along an unplowed road without a center line
or guardrail at the drop-offs, thinking ahead, never

at the precipice. The fir and spruce were prudent,
grave, and meditative, wearing mantles,
bonnets, sleeves of priestly white. Darker clouds
collected at the summits around noon, sending
swirling grapeshot everywhere, erasing forms.
It was primordial, as if pure matter
struggled in a nascent world, or agonized,

diurnal and nocturnal powers clashing at its end.
The combat sputters, dies: as the passes
fall behind me into memory, the road
has opened out onto the rippling tableland, foamy
with snow. I cross the high bridge of the Rio Grande,
with its black abyss, reach Taos. Sharp and still,
the cold has followed, bivouacking in leafless

cottonwoods along the stream and filling spaces
in the heart; but on the mountaintop, the clouds
are tinged with rose and gold, as spirits stir
and walk among the raptured trees, to celebrate
with light and vesperal chant the fullness
of becoming—sage, forest, thought . . . —all,
summoned into presence by the vast and snowy void.

From Denver in a February freeze,
the Colorado First marched south, through drifts,
wind-driven sand, then waves of snow that raged
again. Near Trinidad, our company
joined others, struggling from Fort Wise, and learned
of the disaster in New Mexico:
Confederates with Sibley had prevailed
over Kit Carson's volunteers and men

from Cañon City at Valverde. Well
entrenched, the rebel troops could pause, regroup,
then, northward, move along the Rio Grande
and take Fort Union, opening the West
to the secessionists. In haste, we crossed
the mountains of Ratón, discarding gear
except for arms and blankets, marched all night,
and reached the fort—exhausted, starved, benumbed

by frost. Thank God, we had the time to rest
and wrap our feet, before our officers
decided to set out for Santa Fé.
Debouching from a cañon, we surprised
and fought a party of Confederates—
New Mexicans and Texas Rangers; two
days later, at La Glorieta Pass,
we found their camp. The Southerners were fierce

and well-equipped, and fought ferociously
for seven hours. Outnumbered, we fell back.
Then Chivington decided on a flank
attack, and with five hundred regulars
and volunteers, he climbed a precipice
above the camp, then had the men descend
by rope along the cliff and fall en masse
upon the rebels' rear, as in the fight

at Roncevaux. The wagons and supplies
we'd spotted from the bluff, and burned at once,
the rebels too surprised for quick defense.
It was their last attempt to take the West
for purposes I could not countenance,
if this be true: those other human beings
in bondage, purchased, often beaten, chained.
How strange that mountain men, ungainly birds

attached to cords, and suffering from cold
and want and wounded feet, should liberate
our fellows in the sun of cotton fields.
We barely knew *ourselves*—still less, the war's
ideals. I think that history, in fact,
is not so plain: the good, the evil, clear
at times, yet twisted elsewhere, sticky, dark,
and drawing us into a web of deeds

where consequences cling for many years.
So petty reasons surely held that day,
but great ones too. The dead will not decide,
nor God, until His time is full; for us,
uncertainty, and sorrow that our soldiers died,
and memory of hardship.—In my sleep
I rub my feet and feel the stinging flakes
against my face; I dangle from the cliff

along the cañon where we dropped, or watch
the powder flash, then flame in smoky plumes
as it exploded; once in dream I heard
the lamentations of a woman slave
whose husband had been sold, and then her cries
as, freed, he leapt up on the porch and called
—her heart more violent than mine in space,
her face a blazing aureole of love.

PRICKLY PEAR

It grows in scattered patches on the range,
inventions of the desert in its thirst,
the fibers waiting for a summer change,
the memory of water swelling first.

Ignoring Newton's law, its pads aspire
to opulence beneath patrician blue,
and raise precarious constructions higher,
collapsing when their reason goes askew.

Its countenance is homely, heaven knows,
and innocent enough, until you stand
too near: the inch-long thorns can tear your clothes,
the tiny spines attack an errant hand.

But yellow blossoms graciously atone
for prickliness; the desert bees find sweet
potential in the chalices, and drone
in vectors of mellifluous conceit;

as stock in leanest years can stay alive
consuming pithy stem and even root,
and wanderers of the wilderness survive
in desperation on its knobby fruit.

And here, a nest, concealed, with bits of hair
from flying seeds, and there, a flushing dove
inscribe a sentient presence in the air—
as evidence, in revery, of love.

An edge of shadow startles us; the rain
is still a promise, but the pear and I
distend our porous being, entertain
the wind, and wait upon the potent sky,

where clouds that shimmered in refiner's light
devise refreshment flooding through the scene,
as parched and prickly images take flight,
anticipating, winged, the fields of green.

This is the house that Mabel built—with Antonio,
still a Taos Indian but renamed Tony, and his *Lujan*
written with an *h*, as if she could not quite consent
to the primitive mind, though she sought it, running
from the heights of culture—Tuscany, New York—
and wealth that had provided friends, salons, a villa
done to her design, a Renaissance perfection. Three
adobe rooms opening to a portal, heavy cottonwoods—

great gold, tawny beasts in fall—the Acequia Madre
running through corn, walls dense as dream, Mabel
herself robed in a native weaving: I imagine it now
as she first saw it, close to the earth, ancient enough.
Again, she became idea, drawing outlines in the sand
with a stick, gathering sage and mud for the *latillas*
in the ceilings, buying massive *vigas* and sienna tiles,
letting the spirit move her as she moved her world

in a strange harmony, looking out on Taos Mountain.
There's her solarium, its windows turned four ways,
wisely, like owl's eyes; and the bath, the glassy panels
Lawrence painted, letting in the sun; and Willa Cather
wrote in this small bedroom by the gallery; and here,
O'Keeffe resided, meditating on the Sangre de Cristos,
her head inhabited by flowers, cattle skulls, and cross.
Ah, Mabel! Unlike you, I cannot leave an architect,

nor give up a Tuscan villa, nor marry an artist merely
to use him to get to New Mexico, divorcing him later
for a Tewa Indian; nor is the mountain now so wise—
its eyes unseeing where we do not see. Not the house,
not even its prismatic light, can cure us, but the mind,
holding the vision fast: it preens itself, a bird of indigo
emerging from the ashes, winging upwards, calling out
with hieratic voice and flashing blue among the clouds.

WEAVINGS

Of use, or lovely—they are but material, having
shape and shade and texture and extension
into space, commonly rectangular, and nubby
to the touch, with fringe or whipstitch
edges, or a border, dark; but they are also vision,
revery, desire, hope: the old work of Penelope,

proving with a tapestry undone her constancy,
until it was rewarded; dreams of Navajos
who, driven from their pastures, tasted ashes
but believed that fire would rekindle
in their native hearths; the inner flame of weavers
now, embracing a tradition, knowing beauty,

turning meaning into means. Early Chief's,
Storm Pattern, Two Gray Hills, and Teec Nos Pos—
they are imagination realized in wool, the way
a being is expressed in acts. Nellie John
designed and wove the Two Gray Hills rug hanging
on my wall above a turkey fan; her photograph,

attached, shows eyes of basalt in a well-etched
face, where, as in her handiwork, a vision
is proposed to us, obliquely. I conceive, abstracted
in the earthen colors of the sheep she sheared,
ideas of rock, the pride of Western light,
a thought of hills and clouds; I run my hands

along the nap, desiring its truth—not to possess
it as appropriation, but to apprehend another's
symmetry, to feel the sunrise reddening
her mesa, blue of morning, blue of afternoon,
and sundown tying up the day, her mind in order,
musing on geometries of spirit and of world.

GREAT PINE

Not a soul this summer afternoon at the Kiowa
Ranch, near Taos, except a guardian, an old
curmudgeon of a man, with curt replies
and, I think, a very imperfect understanding
of what Lawrence, Frieda, Brett, O'Keeffe
might have believed, imagined, striven

after. Nonetheless, while admiring the skyline
Lawrence thought the most beautiful
in the world, I try to make conversation, and ask
him about his dog, limping around with a cast
on a foreleg. "Raccoon. Cost me two
hundred bucks at the vet's."—Well, at least

he didn't set the leg himself. Leaving him,
we explore the place on our own—the memorial,
gypsum-white, its truth in azure, phoenix
of gold, and Lorenzo's ashes mixed
in the walls with New Mexico sand; the barn,
the homesteader's cabins, one, Brett's, open,

with barely room for a bed, the other, Lawrence's,
a bit larger, locked and furnished still,
we see, for writing. Suddenly, then, before us,
the great ponderosa pine—my God!
The very tree that Georgia painted, lying
for days under its limbs, seeing it at first perhaps

as polyp, labyrinth, or puzzle, green of foreground
wrestling with turquoise sky, becoming
stylized, whole, filling her vision, as the ideal
took hold of them all. An incantation draws me
to the ancient trunk, the bark a hard and chiseled
bas-relief. The branches reach, immense,

toward the haze, the blue-wrapped mountains,
weaving their way up: fifty feet, a hundred?
I stand among the roots, huge serpents wiser
than the beast of myth, to grasp a lower
limb, pluck off a spray of needles, feel their sharp,
familiar points, and rub the resiny aroma

on my hands. Shaman still, the tree releases
thought like pollen, shaking its huge head, then
returns to its own being, shunning the indifferent—
no phallic passion now to honor it,
no body to lie prostrate before Cybele—the pagan
spirit gone, the genius of desire as still as stone.

A TAOS HYMN

O Spirit of the living God,
O voice of wind, O leavened sod,
made visible in mountains' age,
the water's song, the rippling sage,
dark-shaded canyon, and the whine
of storm through ponderosa pine:
as Christ the Logos hallowed words
of earth—grain, lilies, nesting birds—

and, gesturing toward a desert place,
invoked repose and simple grace,
give benediction to us here
who celebrate the ripened year
in Taos Pueblo's perfect air
with reverence akin to prayer,
admiring golden cottonwoods,
clear river, and these native goods—

retablos, silver, azure stone,
clay vessels, weavings, awls of bone—
whereby belief and weathered hands
did honor to ancestral lands
and to the great Creator's mind,
which shares its power with mankind,
configuring the endless skies,
divinely formed, for human eyes.

So may these artifacts of earth
remain as evidence of worth,
attesting to creation's art
and holy deserts in the heart
whose blue horizons blaze to fire
and shimmer with divine desire,
God held in azimuthal ken,
redeeming us and world. Amen.

I had in mind Georgia O'Keeffe—the cliffs of red
and yellow, sky enormous, lines of vision reaching
out as from her eyes, and the adobe house, anchor
to her painting, to her life—earthen-colored, simple
in its moods, with ladder, bones, and skulls bearing
still her thought's impressions. Well, here's a gate,

with sulfurous hills nearby, streaked in gray; piñon
green and azure deepen as if she too gazed at them.
But then—good heavens!—here's a helicopter pad,
with a chopper rotoring down, beside a tank truck
and a shack; and over there, an asphalt parking lot
holds a hundred campers, cars, RVS, packed in rows

as for a tailgate party. Having come this far, I shall
continue, warily: crunching the gravel, trying to feel
the place's spirit, I arrive at Georgia's house—or *is*
it? This looks newer, vaguely imitative, like a motel,
with another dozen cars: so many pilgrims traveling
for art? No: the ranch has turned into a conference

center, with refectory, accommodations for the night,
and lecture halls; from an open door I hear a speaker
holding forth, I swear, in German—as though truth
could be rhetorical, collective, reached in a gathering,
while Georgia, an alchemist of the ideal, worked all
alone, refining meaning from the silence and the light,

transfiguring the rock, collecting evidence of being.
This is too much for me, oppressive: the house itself,
off limits in the trees, rejoins a mental scene; images
of the hills I'll have to separate from squatting trucks—
abstracting form, as from her mind she drew a single
flower. Going back to Taos, I must stop at Abiquiú

to look at what she had admired there, see the fortress
church, Santo Tomás—solid of design, yet innocent,
its massive hand-hewn *vigas* holding up belief, its tin
retablos and its altar candidly alive with gentle saints.
I drive through San Juan Pueblo, cross the Rio Grande
again, and follow it upstream among the cottonwoods,

now golden in autumnal wealth. Dark wings above
me vivify the field of blue; thistles raise their white
and purple goblets in a toast to beauty. The ghosts
are gone, perhaps, or ride along with me, following
a thought that animated them, clinging to the living
stones of vision, breath across the river, ardent eyes.

GEORGIA'S LADDERS

At Ghost Ranch and Abiquiú, she saw the models
every day, as I see them in the photographs—
fine hand-hewn ladders made of native timbers,
propped against the patio or exterior wall
and reaching past the roof—well-weathered
wood against adobe brown and turquoise sky,

cloud-veined. The ladders took her heavenward
and earthward, as the Mogollon and Anasazi
stepped down in their kivas to the spirit-holes,
then up again, and scaled the cliff sides of the Gila
River basin, Canyon de Chelly, Betatakin,
summoning the gods. She knew the meaning

of the everyday for them, a metaphysics realized
in the visible, as in her canvases; she visited
their sites with six dimensions: compass points
of all four winds, the nether and the upper
spheres, collecting thought. At Ghost Ranch,
alone, she sometimes clambered on the roof

to meditate—or slept there, silvered by the moon
in darkness of obsidian, showered by
the stars she painted at the Lawrence Ranch.
I think of the Chaldean sages studying their destiny
in ordered movements of the constellations—
of the angels Jacob saw ascending and descending

on his visionary ladder; John of Patmos, thirsting
for the Lamb, at twilight may have fled
on housetops to imagine the Apocalypse. Georgia
drew her floating ladder on a plane of green,
above the darkened silhouette of Cerro Pedernal—
halfway between half-moon and earth, a golden

dream of rising bodiless. I reach its horizontals,
grasp its verticals, and all the world expands,
a whirling sphere of light and color, sky connected
to the earth along the ladder's lines of force,
and hills at the horizon in an undulating galaxy,
all rising, phosphorescent, into radiant night.

AT BISHOP'S LODGE

We lunch, well-shaded by a parasol, on a veranda
high above the cottonwoods, the winding road,
with mountains grazing in the distance,
shadow-fringed and mantled in Madonna blue,
looking back at us. So the pastor come
from France into this desert saw them in the summer

through the whitened light of noontide, going in
for his siesta, or in idle moments after morning
prayers, leaving the little hip-roofed chapel
for an immeasurable vault of sky. Even
a vicar apostolic, bishop, then archbishop,
Christ's own emissary to a land half-heathen still,

sought refuge in the hills, casting off the dust
of Santa Fé and riding here on horseback, fleeing
the burros' dung, fetid adobe huts, a child
with swollen belly, eyes like dead birds'—
at nightfall, cries, a knife, and blood. Cooler
air and calm, with wind for company and space

to nourish vision: yet the passion of the wilderness
remained with him, weighting his orisons as
by stones: the weariness of journeys to his flock
dispersed (the Pueblos, Zunis, Hopis, Utes, Paiutes,
and Navajos), the hostile tribes, the sin
and sordidness—as now the world with us, profane,

but heirs-apparent to his refuge, hearing Cather's
words, where something of his ministry
endures, and life defined by an ideal is life well
spent: we move refreshed, imagining, as Lamy
did, a holy presence in the trees, a voice—
a paradise in sage and piñon pine, and in the soul.

RASPBERRIES

The bush has no distinction—common leaves,
sharp spines, dull flowers, spindly canes and stems;
but such indifference of looks deceives:
its berries are, for eye and palate, gems.

Round, grainy, of the deepest ruby red,
they might be pebbles from a jeweled shore,
or tears of blood shed by a dryad, dead
of grief when her beloved loved no more.

Too insubstantial for long delight,
they should be picked, and eaten, in a day—
a glancing smile, a moment's song, a bite
of sugared ecstasy that melts away.

These tender globes, delicious, crushed in cream,
purvey, with flavor, light and color, swirled,
an image of the summer's crimson dream;
my fruited thought illuminates the world.

BLUE SPRUCE, SANTA FÉ

High priests before the snowy tableland,
their boughs outspread as though in offering,
in caps and cloaks of frost the blue spruce stand,
officiants as winter yields to spring.

In sheltered patios, alien redbud blooms;
old apple trees look young again in white;
forsythia erupts in yellow plumes;
and careless tulips opened in the night;

while cottonwoods, despite their armor, keep
hibernal prudence; skeletal, they hold
new fasciae of shoots transfixed in sleep—
green promises of summer, autumn's gold.

For winter will not leave without a show
of force—late fog, raw wind, wet flakes' reprise;
the mountains stir in mantles of fresh snow,
half-visible through tears in sulking skies.

Perennially sober, just, serene,
their bristling needles dense and twilight-dark,
the blue spruce watch the seasons' shifting scene,
great conic beings on a cosmic ark,

and, nearly changeless, wave to bless the change
as whirling world and wheels of time engage
again, conveying us along the range
down river, into riper light and sage.

POTSHERDS

—Near Mesilla, N.M.

A small museum, here: below a Hopi blanket,
striated with sandstone reds, some Mexican
blue glass, two pots, and potsherds on a shelf.
Kin to an amphora, a Taos pueblo vase awaits
the hush of water; candlesticks, chalk-white
and black, propose a light to come. Beyond
the timbered porch and line of cottonwoods,

the sun in patches gambols down the painted
hills, as hawks dive, furrowing the air, to take
a silent bead on prey. Does such being mock
us, saying that our acts will end as they began,
arisen from the kiln of earth? At White Sands,
gypsum dunes like barren loaves provide a bier
for bones of those who suffered in the desert,

beasts and masters met forever in death's yoke
after will could nourish them no more. The pots,
the potsherds have no key; look on them as mute.
If you shatter them, you will not find the image,
but their random dust, and grief, which blows
on us until God wakens us again, his footsteps
printed, dazzling, glazed, upon the giant ergs.

LLANO ESTACADO

South of Tucumcari, east of the Pecos River,
we're driving, in cheery solitude, a good state road
on the high seas of the desert, rolling, choppy here
and there, with mesas all around us, floating
in aurora borealis colors, bits of stringy greenery
like the Sargasso Sea, and prisms of cascading light—
red and violet, blues of shadow at the taluses,
and a horizon blurred in gold and white like Turner's.

We pass by a ranch or two—lone buildings huddled
behind piñon lined as windbreak—and a crossroads,
joining emptiness. It's T-square straight still,
until suddenly, we're rising in a take-off, skeining
the landscape, looping, leveling out—and now
we're planing on the Llano Estacado, featureless,
the marker mesas well behind us. Strange:
one feels becalmed in motion, even as the vector

of desire advances further—as Coronado and his men,
finding nothing in the Zuni lands, nor among
the pueblos of the Rio Grande, turned east to images
of wealth in Quivira, switchbacked up the Llano,
staked the sea of herbage, rode the Cap Rock breakers,
then marched northward till they met
their dark delusion—getting lost on the return,
the Indians having moved the stakes. What mind

can know them as they were, waken as an ensign
raised the cross and staff each morning,
follow soldiers, weary of the ride, some ill or dying,
(wishing—some—that they were home in Spain)
who lifted aching bodies from unyielding ground
to saddle up again? They *were* their suffering,
as they were their greed and lust, but also
love for these wild clouds that went, full-sailed, before

them, and the drover wind, two-bladed, bearing
grains of sand and dark mortality. Their memory
now is light and dry as driftwood, shaped
by age, floating on the blue of thought. The lightness
seizes us, alive, by updrafts toward the heavens
and the great white-robed spirits of the thunderheads,
earth itself a free and winged projectile,
flying us by flaming sun to *llanos* staked with stars.

CHOLLA

The cholla cactus, rarely alone, desires its own kin
as company: here's a small army of them, straggly,
ragtag, to be sure, crossing the range, with camp-
followers of greasewood and mesquite. This year,
the rain gods have been generous: in the chaparral,
the brush looks tender; buffalo and grama grasses,
sage are turning green as vegetables. Yet the cholla,
dark, indifferent against the sand, seem moribund—

until a thought of verdure, just a haze of chlorophyll
that glints a moment in the spotlight sun, proclaims
that they're alive. Such funny fellows, cholla, arms
askew and skinny, gesturing like cartoon characters
in greeting—as if pleased with their unlikely shapes,
their spines and tiny flowers. Down a wash they dip
with me, fording the dry stones, then march up again
in waves of resolution. Here's a crazy cubist figure

sculpted by Duchamp-Villon, its profile multiplied,
stumbling along as the drum major raises his baton;
over there, a teamster with his load of prickly pear;
another cholla holds, a bit unsteadily, a candlestick.
And here am I—a solitary, superannuated cowgirl
of the new millennium, riding the range in my truck,
wishing for company, not knowing if I could endure
it, though. In my eye's ideal, the cholla sign me up

with them, spiky, spindly, yet accommodating; off
we go together—ranks uncertain, but the destination
the horizon. Collecting desert converts, we proceed
toward the farthest ridges, where the sun rays parley
with the streaming rain next door; vast perspectives
follow us, the sky is oceanic, and I pick our bivouac
ahead, a green indemnity against a desiccated heart,
and spiny sentinels patrolling, bearing spears of light.

Curving deep and far, the sky rides away, so far
that thought could lose itself. Driving south
by way of Navajo country and Gallup, we shade
through piñon pine and juniper, then rise
to ponderosa, feathered branches floating
as if free, pushing at the blue. Mountains fall

behind us; mesas ripple in the distance, knowing
space the way a swimmer knows the water.
To the east, El Morro, "place of writing
on the rock," with its Jurassic memory, capped
with sandstone, open to all winds; to the west,
the Zuni lands, propped up against an azure

canvas at the drama's finish. Coronado's dream
was Cíbola and golden cities in the sky—
but there were six, not seven, shining only
with illusion, built of earth and common
stone, their wealth in trade and canyon-bottoms
tilled, and in resistance. From the pueblos

to the mesa tops, and down, and to Corn Mountain
in a flood, the *Ashiwi* fled, abandoning
their kivas, but the holy men still dancing,
plumed and wearing buckskin robes and heads
of beasts, stained berry-crimson, till they bathed
at last in Christ's own blood. I feel the age

of it. As we come round, piñon smoke ascends
above the *hornos* with their heavy bread,
nourishing as breasts. The sunlight splatters
on the mission church; a dusty spirit swirls below
the ragged clouds and at our feet, pulled
by nether powers. I think them now, the braves,

their bows hung up, the women, silent in the dim,
ecstatic light of mass, their bodies rounded,
browned by time. Have we passed by what
they meant? I think so, like the rest
one does not see; it is an aching: all I have never
known—but might, if time were different.

PETROGLYPHS

They are not merely symbols—rather, things
themselves, their soul, their very essence carved
into the stone, because the world was seen
as an embodiment, its being held
in effigy: a parrot poised for flight,

while in his claw he holds a crescent moon
or scythe, to harvest night or reap the gift
of corn; an antelope with planet eyes;
two dancers as kachinas; lizard men;
three Kokopellis, piping; and, along

the canyon of Penasco Blanco, sun
incised in radiance on the wall, with moon
and star, nine-pointed, on an overhang;
and one presiding hand, an astral print—
the artist's signature, the holy sign

of how the universe and men engaged
together in their sacred motions, year
revolving after year—the solar god
declining, then returning to the north,
a supernova blazing through the sky,

the moon appearing, after many turns,
at full between two pinnacles of rock,
and water falling with the season's change,
as child was born and tender shoots confirmed
a vision. Touched as if by memory,

my own hand finds its measure on the stone,
then waves where spirits on the cliff top watch
for rain, or read the azimuth, as night
draws shining petroglyphs for earth's desire—
a lithic promise written in the light.

SAGE

We've settled with the mountains, leaving pine
and spruce to their magnificence of glade,
and reached the sagebrush steppe, along the line
where wilderness of sun replaces shade.

Here's *artemisia tridentata*, quite
the slender plant, supplied with three-lobed leaves,
their tiny hairs deflecting wind and light,
and tears of yellow flowers for one who grieves.

It shows its prudence: shallow roots procure
the run-off in the springtime; deeper taps
can draw from seeps and channels, to assure
its chances in a summer drought, perhaps.

Here's *artemisia rigida,* stiff
and low and silver-green against the glare,
with blackish stem and branch, which give a whiff
of pungent odor to the playa air;

and *salvia dorrii*—fragrant purple sage—
which mollifies a rocky talus view—
the friend of bees, whose whirring wings engage
among the minty whorls of violet blue.

Ahead, the sagebrush measures the plateau
for us, until a sawtooth range appears
in intimate illusion with the snow,
the clouds, and sunlit foothills, formed in tiers

of distant being. Green emotion binds
the muscled landscape to our gaze; we rise,
a desert fretwork sounding, sage and minds
together, in a moment of the wise.

The sky assumes its grandeur fully, here:
along a canyon, cottonwoods are crushed by space,
and ponderosas lose their majesty
to distances; at the horizon, mesas, pulling
our imagination toward their height,
are merely shallow steps into immensity, purpling

in the mind. Even the thunderheads that led
our way today like angels took up
little room: the sky, so vast, acknowledged
them by deepening, but higher still, a blue capacity
rose heavenwards, its emptiness the predicate
of perfect plenitude. As the dazzling

yellow ball descends, a mass of richer clouds
behind us settles on a ridge, half-dark,
half-light, as rays, inclining, reach its fringes.
Something buzzes—a cicada?—and rustlings
in the desert willow follow the invisible. We wait:
the swollen sun seems motionless,

suspended in the thought of red. The clouds
grow darker . . . denser . . . —then, stained
rose and deep vermilion, pour at last
their molten burden on the mesa tops, the taluses,
the river, as the elements exchange their being—
draperies of water flowing, crimson, down

the shadowed wash, the very flood aflame,
the dust, awakened now and borne
among the raindrops, whirling, incandescent,
in the desiccated wind, the ferrous earth turned
liquid—all the firmament on fire,
streaming with Christ's radiant, dripping blood.

It's on a whim: why not drive on a bit, cross
into Arizona, see the Painted Desert
and the old men of the forest, turned to stone?
What's another hundred twenty miles?
We'll whip down then along the Little Colorado,
pass Lyman Lake and Eagar, work our way
eastward through the San Franciscos,
getting our mountain fix before we flatten out

to feel those long, uninterrupted sands along
the border. Just ahead begin the Painted Cliffs,
rippling in rose and russet and vermilion,
breaking, the way the surf gives out,
then recommencing from the desert swell.
We reach the park, drive north to the museum,
look far toward Lithodendron Wash
and gaze upon the badlands—banded, rouged,

mascaraed, powdered, ready for performance
in the cosmic show. Looping around,
we've got the Puerco Pueblo, Newspaper Rock,
the Teepees, and Blue Mesa, blanched out
by the zenith sun, their ruins honored
with a split-rail fence, a walkway, scattered
reconstructions. For the Anasazi, as they scaled
a precipice like lizards, flew across

the mesas on deer feet, caught the summer rains
in potholes on the slickrock, was there ever
time to marvel at the fallen deities around them—
living beings petrified as they might be—
time, inside the rooms of their survival,
to take joy, as we do now, in colors,
keep them in their minds against the darkness,
think the wondrous, red-dyed world as glory?

The grains propose the spectrum of the landscape (golden,
ochre, glassy, iron red, black of basalt), sorted, sifted.
In his furrowed palms the artist holds the sunlight's
glint, admires coolness poured from earthen jars. With
a willow stick, he sketches on the ground until idea takes

shape. A hawk on steady currents circles, dips, and dives;
at play, a boy picks up a pinecone, turns it in his hand,
and casts it, lightly, carrying his thought, among the trees.
The underlayer of the painting shaped, compressed,
the man then drips the crystal granules in geometries

of mind's design, for mind's enchantment and the eye's,
yet born in nature: mountains, river, mesas, birds,
the sun and stars, changed into lines and circles, triangles,
the z's of storm—commending by world's matter
God's primordial words. The artist pauses, straightens

edges, steps away, seeing his handiwork in its gratuity—
an offering to others, to the day's divinities: what could be
more sacramental than to borrow the earth, reshape
and order it, returning it to earth as a diurnal sacrifice?
The work, perfected, moves toward its undoing as the sun

above the distant mesa waits immobile, swelling like
a woman's body and inflamed, then plunges down,
leaving a ruddy afterbirth. In shadow now, the picture
is erased by him who made it, who himself is dust—bound
to heaven's motions, honoring God's time by dying in it.

DUST DEVIL

What young demiurge, discovering his powers,
sent this spinning top of powder twisting,
spiraling across the sand, outsized, devouring soil,
taunting us at the horizon, pausing in place
as if to catch its breath, then ricocheting
back and whirling on, escaping toward the distant

Navajo plateau? It is unsettling, this epiphany
of air in orange and ochre dust, disheveled, angry,
centrifuged. I follow it, a desert genie
whisking the china blue of sky, the coral cliffs,
and watch it rise, at last, the way a ghostly
presence might blow off, a bit unstable, losing

shape, while, far above, thin clouds of angels'
breath, carded by the upper currents, float
ethereally. The Anasazi, also, watched the stratus
drape the mesa tops and anticlines, wing
east to sail among great monolithic birds
of black basalt, or hover, moored by stillness,

over canyons—watched, too, as arroyos, gouged
by downpours, sank, dissolving earth and stranding
corn, when rain gods sent a year's worth
in a day, then went away. It is the same dust
now, older by a thousand summers, ground
more finely by improvidence. A devil forms again,

playing off past the Paria River, running into pure,
consuming light. What is a life? A moment's
turbulence, a body borrowed by wind—
or deep soil, pools where sun is sieved, and weirs
to hold the run-off, channeling its spirit
into grain and blades of grass and green ideas?

PLUMS

They're Santa Rosas, crimson, touched by blue,
with slightly mottled skin and amber flesh,
transparently proposing by their hue
the splendor of an August morning, fresh

but ruddy, ripening toward fall.—"So sweet,
so cold," the poet said; but this one's tart,
its sunny glow perfected in deceit,
as emulation of a cunning heart.

I eat it anyway, until the pit
alone remains, with scattered drops of juice,
such sour trophies proving nature's wit:
appearances and real in fragile truce.

GRAND STAIRCASE

I'm wrestling with this stair-step wilderness, pushed out
from the sculptor's block of Chaos: eons' matter
scraped and lifted, madly folded, fired, wind-eroded,
water-gouged. What's left is maelstrom, howling,
turbulent in rock, which swirls and breaks and gnarls
within a jumbled labyrinth of gullies, blackened, yellow,

iron-red, with goblin hoodoos in palaver, sawtooth ridges,
cracked plateaus, contorted junipers, gaunt piñon
pines. It's no-man's land; I'm barely hanging on, losing
the topography of thought to naked earth—a twisted
psyche, scarred with wounds and complexes—
and seeing my familiar body, written in the temporal,

mocked by immemorial skeletons of stone: dark sockets,
heavy brows, a backbone as a highway, arcing ribs
and shoulders squared in Titans' labor, elbows,
knots, and knobby knees. I try to deal with the impression,
center it, devise an axis. Playing with idea, I breach
the dunes, concede a point to troughs, spill over breakers

down a switchback road, ascend, then ride a crest, towed
out, imagining a lover calling. Is this what I wanted—
roughness, density, opaque resistance? It is worth
two thousand miles of driving and desire, if my eye
can gather up the landscape in its strangeness,
smooth it out and name it: for a moment, mind adheres

to things, connects along a talus, tests the blue of sky,
and slides toward essences, but glances off and ricochets
into a canyon, yielding to the stubborn stuff
of world—when I should wish for words to curve
around phenomena, fit close, embracing form
and substance in a flash—idea, thing, and sound identical.

II

Later, I remember how a shaft of moonlight, years
ago—a perfect parallelogram framed by a balcony—
visited us in a seaside room; how, when the moon
moved, the blanched light reached the bed, whitely
pouring on the white of sheets and wrapping round
our limbs, oblique, illuminating shadows of desire,

becoming love, the thing itself in shape and sense;
and murmured words as motions took on presence—
nightgown tossed in silvered spiral, falling loose;
two creamy roses, radiant, in a vase, casting being
on the wall; hands, lips, hair commingled—gliding
toward disclosure, smooth, transparent, luminous.

This country is coarse cloth, folded roughly, crumpled,
crushed, or cut in pieces; I'm the needle,
threaded with desire, stitching it together by my eye,
using the center line. As I try to reason with it,
sort it out—sew Boulder Mountain to Grand Staircase,
Bryce, the Markagunt Plateau, Zion, then Nevada—

the folds resist, unyielding, multiplied; I'm barricaded,
patience, nerves, and time the only means
of plying through: creep down an anticline, straddle
backbone ridges, cross a cindered badland, climb
a checkered mesa, mole along a tunnel, skein
the switchbacks, drop into the park. It's not mirage;

I've got two days, before another desert run. What green
reward awaits? Severe, the patriarchs of sandstone
loom; great ponderosas keep their distance; piñon pine
and weathered juniper, hunkering in the upper
crevices, look petrified. In Zion Canyon, though,
beside the North Fork of the Virgin River, looping,

lolling through an ancient lake bed, meadows shimmer,
cool with reeds and willows; pools devise
ideas of emerald; manganese and iron run-offs streak
the cliffs near hanging gardens, watered
by the seepage—yellow, fuchsia, coral flowers,
leafy trains. Upstream, the walls close in, herding

cottonwoods and shadowing the current; in a round,
monolithic domes like Sacré-Coeur rise whitely.
Here, the road gives out. On foot, I reach
the buttresses and listen, cloistered, to the plain chant
of the river stones—then at the narrows, step
into the nave. Quiet and disquiet both: a cloudburst

would engulf the canyon, drowning everything; a single
rock, dislodged, contains my death; the dizzying
verticals give neck-cramps. Yet this is what
I wished to see, after the bath of barrenness,
the unrelenting light. So it is a choice of hermitage:
of sun or shade, a dry lament, a harsh and treeless

vision in the wilds, or refuge in a glade, but deepening,
and no escape save sky. Well, that's the price,
the body in its risks, its possibilities, the self alive
in antinomian illumination, always drawn
to the contrary world—as presence, passage, threshold
into being, with its wilds of sun, its dark, its vertigo.

STILLWATER MARSH

—Lahontan Valley

It shivers, a grisaille, in pensive haze,
then brightens to an opalescent glass,
as winds, conceding sun, revise their ways,
dividing clouds and shimmering the grass.

A million years ago the valley filled
with virgin waters of the Pleistocene;
and beasts of marvel wandered as they willed
among the forests of this vast demesne.

Then men came later from the northern zone
to camp by shrunken remnants of the lake,
where shards of sacred vessels, shells, and stone
left evidence of vision in the brake.

And now the birds descend along the edge
by tens of thousands, tethering their flight,
and cry with feathered language through the sedge
before they reach the moorings of the night.

The distant knolls turn shadowy, and all
the being of the marsh collects in thought—
old seas, the lithic men, the birds' wild call,
embodied moments where the dust is caught—

connecting desert dwellers to their grace,
as when the wanderers, pursuing rain,
invoked the spirits of a greener place,
dropped sacrificial tears upon the plain,

and watched the liquid manna flow, like blood
of women, fertile, mingling with the fire,
that we too, latter children of the flood,
might find the world alive to our desire.

JOSHUA TREES

Undifferentiated, rippling lines
of earthen colors in a sea of haze
between the sky, blanched out at noon,
and saltbush at our feet: the landscape runs
ahead of us in waves, until it fades
at the horizon. To the north, a ridge
of mountains sleeps, its foothills rounded close
in woman's form. The hours pass fully,

deep in possibilities.—Instead, the same
illusions of the road as we resume
our journey after lunch, the monotone
of riffling wind, the range identical;
but later, intimations come of change—
a bluer tone ahead and shadows shaped
toward meaning. Distant figures animate
the scene—a gathering of dervishes,

a dream of hermits in their loneliness?
At last—for it is they—the Joshua trees
appear, their prophets' raiments rough and worn,
their arms upraised as if to supplicate,
enjoin, rebuke ungodliness, or give
their benediction to the alien land
and those who walked across it seeking signs,
the desert opening to their belief

like waters parted. Cactus here and there
collect the prism of the afternoon
in holy blossoms, yellow, purple, red,
below the Joshuas' praying limbs; the vast
and cratered wilderness inclines to thoughts
of paradise, with showers scrimming down
far westward where we gaze, and broken spears
of light announcing grace and green reprieve.

We had traversed a cursèd place, something like hell:
sand hills with no green, half-crusted by a film of salt;
volcanic rocks, grotesquely jagged from primeval fire;
gullies, deep and rugged; scattered sagebrush, holding
onto life but little life to spare. The mules and horses,
pawing, found a bit of forage, but there were no birds
or rabbits. This was at the turning of the year, a Janus
in despair, gazing each way toward wilderness. We ate

some sour jerky and dried peas, our last. Several mules
gave out that day. The next, we wakened to an icy fog,
and, blinded, fought to find the other animals, at picket,
and each other. Climbing up, we finally made our way
along a range of whitish granite, bearded by the winter,
where we camped. That night, the fog dispersed a while,
revealing stars enough to bring us back from desperation,
and at daybreak shimmered on the granite in the coral

alpenglow. Three days: a desert at the mountains' foot,
dry creeks, a desiccated lake, fires of spindly sagebrush,
cold our very being. Snow began to fall by twilight; I
remember one poor animal who tore a hobble, stumbled
to the fire, and lay down, its hide against the heated rock,
its eye a world of agony and wild revulsion. Shuddering,
it died. The destiny of all was written there, I thought,
our hands and feet conceding to the frost, strength spent,

and stones for bread. To stay, to leave . . . The landscape
changed; one afternoon we reached a spring where snow
had melted from telluric heat. We washed our wounded
feet, and drank the saline flow; the animals could graze,
and there was game. My body, aching, yielded to relief,
acknowledging familiar earthen feelings, thinking even
for a moment of my wife, and what delivers us to love.
Again that night I watched the sky, the streaming galaxy,

and took our bearings by the constellations, pasturing.
Much later, we turned westward, with the great Sierra
shouldering the clouds. Whatever might await us there,
little in my life would match, I thought, the desolation
of that igneous plain behind us now, the chthonic dunes,
the company of death, contested, quickened by a granite
watershed at dawn and waves of stars above the spring—
grace having followed us so far along our dark desires.

BRISTLECONE PINES

—In the southern Snake Range

They are the old men of the forest, of the world—
gnarled, wizened, stripped of all the inessentials,
living longest in the heights, along the borders
with the iron sky, embracing cold. Their being,
granite-hard, is dense enough to break a blade;

their limbs and torsos writhe, the sculpted flesh
as twisted as Laocoon. Below, the mountains fall
away into the basin; rivers snake, then disappear
in alkaline oblivion; the greasewood flats reach on
to the horizon. Everything seems vain—the rocks,

memorials to nothingness; the wind, a mockery.
Or do the pines remember us, companions—recall
how Jedediah Smith was fed by Indians on rushes
near their grove, and Lehman hammered through
the mountain's hollow limestone heart, to find

his predecessors there—or Frémont, following
a vision westward, gazed on the Great Basin?
And will they forgive, compassionate, the ones
who immolated here an ancient, venerable tree,
to violate its core and count the five millennia

recorded in its circles? But the druid spirits weep,
I think; the nymphs and sylvan deities still mourn
their forest elders, grown already before Greece
was young—those ravaged boughs dismembered
on the stone, Iphigenia sacrificed in greatest age.

I had not thought to fight a war. It's true
I am an officer, but sent out West
to survey and explore and file reports,
not wage campaigns. And endless land we saw,
my men and I, like nomads on the steppes
of Asia—moving faster, though, across
a hostile country, where the rivers bled
into the barren earth, as whirls of sand

concealed the sun, and hogback ridges ran
in breastworks, bristling, one ridge behind
another, till we reached the snowy range
of pickets westward. Racked by cold and wind,
we nearly missed the pass. At last, we came
down to the valleys, desperate for food,
a dram of warmth, and horses to replace
our broken mounts. When war with Mexico

looked imminent, we joined the fray, enrolled
by circumstance or will—my Delawares,
the Walla Walla scouts, Kit Carson, all
deployed to fight the *Californios*.
We sometimes slept in beds, at Sutter's Fort
and settlers' farms, and ate a proper meal,
or lay in sheets of cold on rocky ground ˙
along those marches, north and south and back

again. You know what happened: ragtag troops
and converts meeting, by design or flaw
of plan, in skirmishes, with many killed
and others left to die, and little clear
except that we dislodged the occupants
from various towns and finally held the coast
as well. I thought of Hector and Achilles, kin
in epic combat, honorable both—

and of Andromache, the dark-eyed wife—
like one who came into my room that day
in San Luis Obispo, dressed in black,
escorted by a guard. The square was lush
with fragrant lemons, fig trees, soughing palms;
but in his cell her husband, Don Jesús,
our prisoner, accused of treachery,
was waiting to be shot. She knelt and begged

me for his life. We all had seen enough
of hardship, and consumed the bitter bread
of death on both sides; too, my wife and child
were always in my mind. I had him brought
to me. He held himself with dignity, quite pale,
but noble. When I pardoned him, he cried,
"God gave me one life: you have granted me
a second. I am yours." The other men

we'd captured were set free and joined our band,
and all of them proved loyal in our last
encounters. Those heroics, if they were,
are done, no Homer to relate them now;
but I remember how the sunlight breached
the shutters, shining on a milky way
of tears, and birds sang out to break the glass
of stillness as Andromache arose.

KACHINAS

They are the ancient essence of the world,
of animals and plants, of water, stones—
who dwell six months in nether darkness, swirled
among telluric powers, roots, and bones.

Then, at the winter solstice, they appear,
embodied in the Hopis' ritual dance,
and live as desert men for half a year,
assuming as their own the human chance.

In feathered costumes, masked, with painted eyes,
and shaking rattles formed of squash and maize,
they urge the sluggish deity to rise,
soliciting the light of longer days.

By June, the earth is ripe, the dancing done;
the spirits slip into the underground,
entrusting to the clouds and guardian sun
the green abode of being, turning round.

Their images remain: admire how
these figures, fashioned from a weathered heart
of cottonwood, connect me to them now,
through emblematic presence of their art,

as they devise for me in ritual mime—
inhabiting by grace this middle field—
the meeting of the mesa tops and time,
embracing sacred dark and starry shield.

MESQUITE

A brash conception of the chaparral,
mesquite excels in notion and design,
with leafy opulence, and rationale
of being realized in every line.

Where parching air and potency of noon
would desiccate and scorch a piney glade,
mesquite draws deeply, and from opportune
extravagance of sun devises shade.

In amorous commotion, nesting birds
make reason from the tangle of its limbs,
and resined winds of spring, eschewing words,
along its supple shoots compose their hymns;

while, water witchers of the arid range,
the roots, great muscled arms, investigate
a hydra's head of channels, to exchange
their porous patience for a liquid freight.

So in their dark connections, all the good
and whirling of the elements conspire
to be transformed into a feat of wood,
which in its turn will kindle as our fire;

that in the wilderness no lesser mind
may grow than by a garden's greenest zeal,
the rough materials of the world refined,
and branches multiplied to the ideal.

CANYON WRENS

They are the music of the wilderness, sounding
through the redrock boulders, singing in antiphony
among the cliffs, the draws, the cottonwoods—
swooping from secret clefts of slickrock as they call,
perching where the Anasazi and the Mogollon
left memories in caves and monoliths, finding

a foothold where a holy man ascended toward
the sky. In their notes, something like joy takes hold
of me, putting to shame a touch of *ennui;* wings
glinting dark against the blue, I rise and soar
with them, alighting then to gather sticks and grass,
seeking a hidden place along the stream or rocks,

and weaving into a rough architecture immemorial
meaning.—There, above the ponderosa, halfway
up the canyon walls, they fly, a pair! And here
another planes, makes arcs over the abyss, and dives,
its russet flashing on the green, into the shadow
of a grove of piñon pine, its disembodied voice

outpouring to the earth its inmost being. How can
we know the world, except by such attentions,
calling out the presence and the power of what *is,*
surpassing all the human sense of purpose—
letting the old questions dangle in the wind, unwanted,
Why, why? blown away, silenced by *I sing, I sing.*

Notes

"Enos Mills on the Divide": Information in this poem comes from Mills's book *The Spell of the Rockies* (Boston and New York: Houghton Mifflin, 1911).

"Stratton's Gold": Information on Winfield Scott Stratton comes from Marshall Sprague, *Newport in the Rockies* (Denver: Sage Books, 1961).

"Conejos Rising": The composer alluded to is the American Benjamin Boretz; his statement is quoted by Alex Ross, *New Yorker*, 6 June 2005, 100.

"La Glorieta": Details about the march and engagement at La Glorieta come from Eugene Parsons, *The Making of Colorado: A Historical Sketch* (Chicago: A. Flanagan, 1908).

"A Taos Hymn": It may be recalled that in Mark 6:31, Christ invites the apostles to rest in a desert place.

"Georgia's Ladders": The photographs referred to include one by Malcolm Varon and one by John Loengard, reproduced in Britta Benke, *Georgia O'Keeffe, 1887–1986* (Cologne: Taschen, 2000), 79, 80, respectively; and three by Robert Reck, in *Architectural Digest*, March 2002, 180, 187, 188. The paintings referred to are *The Lawrence Tree* (1929) and *Ladder to the Moon* (1958).

"Petroglyphs": The "pinnacles of rock" are those at Chimney Rock in southern Colorado. Every 18.6 years, the moon rises between the two pinnacles in what is called a lunar standstill.

"Sage": The genus *Artemisia* (sage) was named to honor the bereaved widow of Mausolus, who built for him the great Mausoleum at Halicarnassus. An earlier Artemisia accompanied Xerxes in his invasion of Greece and distinguished herself in the battle of Salamis by her prudence and courage. The name is derived from that of Artemis, the huntress. Purple sage, which has a minty-sage aroma, is related to sagebrush only distantly by division and class, but shares much of the same territory.

"Frémont in the Granite Range" and "Frémont in California": Details about the explorations of John Frémont and the fighting in California come from Ferol Egan, *Frémont: Explorer for a Restless Nation* (New York: Doubleday, 1977; rpt. Las Vegas: University of Nevada Press, 1985).

"Bristlecone Pines": In the cave alluded to, now named for Absolom Lehman, Lehman discovered bones known to be those of Native Americans.